Praise f

I Done Clicked My H...

"So many of the greatest poets in the American tradition have been Chicago Black women, and this debut collection is an announcement that one more has joined that proud tradition. Byas's work unfolds with tender attention to all sides of life in the Black metropolis. From mulberry trees to daisy dukes to candy ladies to liquor stores, this work sings of the city that raised me in an authentic way, with a careful formal attention befitting the lineage of Gwendolyn Brooks. This is a work to cherish."

—NATE MARSHALL, author of *Finna: Poems*

"My fellow Chicagoans, rejoice. Taylor Byas's poems are visually stunning and formally inventive. They give us more proof that everything dope does indeed come from Chicago."

—JOSÉ OLIVAREZ, author of *Promises of Gold*

"In *The Wiz*, Dorothy finds the song of Oz and follows it down the road, easily—it is the song of her spirit, Tin Man's heart, Scarecrow's brain, Lion's bravery. It is a city revealing what is already there inside those travelers. Taylor Byas unearths that spirit-music, too, in her stunning debut, *I Done Clicked My Heels Three Times*. These poems illuminate Chicago, the body, the sweat of condensation on the Kool-Aid cups cooling in the heat on a summer day in technicolor memory and careful music. It is the Chicago that's there all along among the emerald streets, the self that is always there—a voice behind the curtain shouting I'm here, listen! It is the loud and frightening sparkle of a father's memory and the sharp edge of a lover's rough touch. It is the shades of love blooming, green, across the South Side of Chicago. In fresh, inventive, and living formal verse and free verse, Taylor Byas paints the golden path, brick by brick, and we ease on down it."

—ASHLEY M. JONES, author of *Reparations Now!: Poems*

"Some collections attempt to build new worlds. Others return to old worlds and write them anew. Byas's dive into the familial and the familiar is an intimate project, one that questions motherhood, love, and mourning in tandem. All this, in a Chicago that shole ain't what this world tries to make of it. Byas's Chicago flexes and bristles and brims with life. In Byas's work, Chicago is a/the world, one reimagined as a clever, raw, and beautiful character. Clever, especially so because Byas uses a vast tool belt stocked well with forms and voice(s) and smirking candor. She tells us off and tells us the truth. Byas writes, 'what we want has so little room to grow,' yet all the while makes room, makes room, makes room. Move out the damn way already!"

—AURIELLE MARIE, author of *Gumbo Ya Ya: Poems*

Praise for *Bloodwarm*

"There is no escaping. There is no hiding. There is only you and the page and the hauntings that Taylor Byas brings forth in each poem. *Bloodwarm* is a book that chills the spine, yes, but also meditates on the now. We are at a gas station. We are on Twitter. We are leaving a voicemail for Madam C. J. Walker. Through rhythm, repetition, and rapport, Byas weaves together poems that will decor the night, while we sit in a dark corner counting to ten then screaming 'ready or not, here I come.' And although we seek, it is her words that find us." —LUTHER HUGHES, founder of Shade Literary Arts

"I trust Taylor Byas with language; her poems are giving, durable, flexible, and her debut chapbook collection *Bloodwarm* is no different. Byas offers a complex blend of form and free verse in between each poem as she scavenges for a space she can call safe for the Black woman. Byas writes, 'But my black ass would never be / in Spiderman's grip. My "damsel-in-distress" / don't look like Kirsten Dunst or Emma Stone—I looked.' This collection is a mirror of the Black experience through the murder, erasure, and displacement of Black people in the world and how Byas hopes to one day save us all." —JASON B. CRAWFORD, author of
Summertime Fine and *Twerkable Moments*

"Taylor Byas gets to the bone of it. In *Bloodwarm*, Byas illuminates Blackness and the ways in which this country is riddled with a violent colonial gaze and a thirst for Black blood, even in the grocery store, at the gas station, on the night roads of Alabama in a sundown town, in the cage of a pantoum, the ease of a sonnet, the revelatory erasure. These poems are exact in their questioning— Byas gives the reader a beating heart on each page, even when that heart is stopped by a policeman's gun or by the slur thrown into a speaker's back. There is a 'gift [of] fire' in these pages. Byas, unrelenting, ignites us all."
—ASHLEY M. JONES, author of *Magic City Gospel*,
Dark // Thing, and *Reparations Now!*

Praise for *Shutter*

"In *Shutter*, 'each frame makes a stranger of' not just strangers, but of the selves we bracket, the language we tend with hands and tongues. Byas deploys double exposed syntax and the unflinching accuracy of film, turning page after phrase to create a gallery of the illumination and development survival demands of any woman, but especially Black women with the audacity to exist, dream, and unwrap themselves for the possibility of a love that is not consumption. A love letter to desire and its attendant dangers, *Shutter* does not quiver 'in nosy moonlight,' it stands in the doorway seductively, daring you to expose yourself."

—JENI DE LA O, *The Poetry Question*

I DONE

Clicked My Heels

THREE TIMES

ALSO BY TAYLOR BYAS

Bloodwarm
Shutter

I DONE
Clicked My Heels
THREE TIMES

Poems

Taylor Byas

Soft Skull   New York

First Soft Skull edition: 2023

Grateful acknowledgment for reprinting materials is made to the following: Claudia Rankine, ["Some years there exists a wanting to escape–"] and ["February 26, 2012 / In Memory of Trayvon Martin"] from *Citizen: An American Lyric*. Copyright © 2014 by Claudia Rankine. Reprinted with the permission of The Permissions Company, LLC on behalf of Graywolf Press, graywolfpress.org.

Library of Congress Cataloging-in-Publication Data
Names: Byas, Taylor (Poet), author.
Title: I done clicked my heels three times : poems / Taylor Byas.
Identifiers: LCCN 2023000848 | ISBN 9781593767419 (trade paperback) | ISBN 9781593767426 (ebook)
Subjects: LCGFT: Poetry.
Classification: LCC PS3602.Y33 I25 2023 | DDC 811/.3—dc23/eng/20230106
LC record available at https://lccn.loc.gov/2023000848

Cover design by Farjana Yasmin
Cover illustration of chicago skyline © iStock / Caratti
Book design by tracy danes

Published by Soft Skull Press
New York, NY
www.softskull.com

Printed in the United States of America

10 9 8 7 6 5 4 3 2 1

To the south side of Chicago
and to every place and person that has been
home to me since I left you

And she has a name for the moan that worries gently in her hair. It is called Chicago.

—PATRICIA SMITH, "The Awakening,"
Life According to Motown

Contents

Section I: The Feeling That We Have

Section II: Can I Go On?

Section III: Poppy Girls

Section IV: Ease on Down the Road

Section V: Emerald City Sequence

Section VI: Is This What Feeling Gets?

Section VII: Believe in Yourself

SECTION I

The Feeling That We Have

South Side (I)

This is what teaches me love. Your streets, their wailing
for their dead. The way a siren becomes a mother
too. How my parents hold me like some frail thing
to their chests at night, how quick they are to cover

my ears when the block gets hot. The handshake half-hug
sacred enough to make a man feel whole
again. The shapeshifting, how what looks like a thug
in darkness softens into a boy in the gold-

glow of a bedside lamp. How we are all
somebody's grandbaby. Harold's Chicken steeped
in so much hot sauce, the nose runs, and the small
piece of bread too wet to hold, drowning beneath

the fries. Each of our brownstones, side by side—
so there's nowhere to run, nowhere for us to cry.

Blackberrying

after Sylvia Plath

> Blacker the berry, sweeter the juice
>
> —EDMONIA HENDERSON, "Black Man Blues"

Children in the yard, and nothing, nothing but blackberries,
blackberries culled from the waist-high bushes, the blister-bumps
smashed down to seed and muck, then handprints on white
button-downs and knee-highs. Blackberries pricked by thumbnail,
an accidental murder, my own miscalculation of what the black skin
could endure. Blackberries slit then quickly squished, berrying
down the sides of my fingers, wet splints for the joints.
I could not tell if my mother's sighed requiem was for the fruit
or my ruined clothes. Perhaps she lamented the deep red stain

on my hands, mistaken for the first sample of womanhood. The next
week, children exhausting from school buses, flocking
to the bushes in the yards to blackberry again. Us little Black girls
crowning our fingers, blackberries for acrylic nails, for cat claws.
The little Black boys lugging the white plugs from the fruit's center
like grenade pins, throwing them across the yard before diving
headfirst into grass. We could only fight temptation for so long.

We grind the berries in our palms again, let the juice tattoo
new veins down to elbow pit, lap up the pulp with our tongues.
We paint our faces berry-black, the careless dashes like freedom
papers, releasing us from something we don't yet understand.
The evenings always end in taste—the sweet syrup drying like
   blood on our lips.

Corner Store

Fluorescent red and yellow letters stutter
FAIR DISCOUNT: LIQUOR SOLD HERE. Metal bars
cover glass, the owner's slapdash notes
on the entrance—USE THE OTHER DOOR, NO SHIRT
NO SHOES NO SERVICE—Sharpied on the backs
of old receipts. These aisles I can't forget;
the quarter bags of chips I'd buy and flip
for profit in our sock-rot locker rooms,
the frosted glass doors with their fingerprints
and drinks I dreamed to taste-test on porch steps.
Older men who gummed out *baby girl*, with smoke
and corn chip breath they offered like candy.

I ain't your baby girl, your sweet thang, your
nothing. At checkout, the man before me
opens his 40, takes a swig while paying,
pays extra to cover my chips, my juice,
the fear that flowers in my belly when
he slaps my ass, follows me halfway home.

The First House

There are no gardens for our brownstones,
only the square bite of courtyard

out back, three other buildings sidling up
like dinner guests. Only split sidewalk

fringing a tuft of dead grass, enough
space for Little Tikes tricycles and

the rats' monthly meetings. Even the walls,
half-pint, forever child-sized,

my bedroom ceiling yawing downward
like the underside of a playground slide

or seesaw. Our kitchens stacked like Legos.
What we want has so little room to grow.

*

Still, some things creep through the cracks.

The weeds in the small backyard, those
thick, pill-bodied roaches and their

choreographed promenades
on the other side of the walls,

their eventual spawning in the wool
of my house shoes. And the limp-wristed

wrangling of gunfire out front, bullets
like punctuation—beginning and ending more

than sound—until a stray pricks our front
window, anchors down in the stuffing

of my father's favorite recliner. Days later,
I would dig into the hole, not to recover

the bullet, but to feel an open wound.
To know what it means to cheat death.

When the Air-Conditioning Breaks

We discover home-grown auto-tune and yawp
our Vaselined lips mere inches from the box fan's
lattice—the flowered blades compute and swap
our breaths for robot, monotone. When our friends

sardine the porch and ask, *Y'all coming out?*
we let the screen door boomerang back to chop
the wooden frame, our dizzy laughter cutting out
our grandmother's kitchen edict—*Close that door and stop*

letting my air out this house. All bark, no bite.
When we return, our shadows race the sunset
back to the earth. Inside, we doff our white
tank tops and blue jean shorts, our naked silhouettes

like trophies welded in summer's afterburn,
hot metal cooling to things for her to love—to spurn.

The Early Teachings

The Catholic school says, *Cover your shoulders*
because the boys may be tempted by your flesh.

Because the boys may be tempted by your flesh,
your safety is your responsibility.

Your safety is your responsibility
at the party you didn't want to go to.

At the party you didn't want to go to,
a white tablet dissolves into your drink.

A white tablet dissolves into your drink
and no one believes that you told him no.

And no one believes that you told him no—
it's your responsibility, remember?

It's your responsibility. Remember,
the Catholic school says, *Cover your shoulders.*

You from "Chiraq"?

I say I'm from Chicago and
    folks get excited. I mean, they
light up like they got gossip to tell.
    But really, they think they got me
figured all the way out. They say, *You*
    from Chiraq? Once, a follow-up—*Are*
you a gangsta?—as he extended a crooked
    hand, pointed his finger-gun at my face, and
curled his thumb for the air-soft trigger. I
    stared down the barrel of his hand, gave the answer
I'm sure he wanted to hear, said *Yes,*
    I'm a hard-ass, don't fuck with me, and it
was a lie, I know. But so is
    everything else he believes to be true
about me and the South Side. And yeah I
    almost held a bullet in my hands, have
taken cover among broken glass. I've seen
    kids' bicycles whizzing down the block as the
streetlights came on. I've even seen a gunman
    double-fisting glocks on my street. But he ain't kill
nobody. I had friends on that block and
    a boy who nicknamed me every time he would go
past my building. My happiness was free,
    or 25 cents when the candy lady came to
my street. So when the next person asks, I kill
    all that noise. *It's Chicago, and I'm no gangsta. Don't say it again.*

Jeopardy! (The Category Is Birthright)

List of potential correct answers submitted

For $200: When inheritance begins

    What is: in the womb
    What is: decades before I announced my father dead
        to me
    What is: twenty-four years before I knew that everything passed
        down ain't good ain't gold
    What is: when my mother was a crucifix
        in the hospital bed, split open
    What is: when her memory of that pain becomes
        my first heirloom, scrubbed clean
        from her body's memory
    What is: when I was a blood-spangled lotus in the doctor's
        gloves, given my father's last name
        before even my mother could claim it

For $400: Nurture vs. Nature

    What is: blood is thicker than water vs. blood type
    What is: how to make onion gravy to smother porkchops vs.
        being smothering
    What is: how to drive my father's truck vs. how I drive
        people out of my life with my fear
        of the past re-pouring itself another glass
    What is: to avoid eye contact because it leaves me feeling
        a little too raw vs. eye color
    What is: my disgust for liquor vs. my penchant for sweet wine,
        for vodka and cranberry juice, for
        a strong Long Island
    What is: how to hate my father vs. loving him still

For $600: If my father is an alcoholic, then I must be _____

What is: careful
What is: suspicious of every man's thirst for anything
    he can't drink from me
What is: afraid of the way I slow down in the wine
    aisle at Walmart
What is: learning how to uncork a bottle of Champagne
    because it feels like a necessary skill to have
What is: fascinated by how a frozen bottle of liquor behaves
    like a body just dead, the outside frosting faster
    than the inside
What is: choosing to never take a drink in front of my
    mother because I remind her of him enough
    as it is

For $800: What people mean when they say I am "my father's
child"

What is: we look alike
What is: time filled my purse with parts of him whether
    I wanted them or not
What is: I got the same grape-swollen cheeks, his button nose
    sewn onto the geography of my face
What is: if I drink a lick of liquor, I can almost taste how bitter
    he got
What is: my love need be like a religion, my tolerance that
    of Jesus, how I should learn to turn the other
    cheek before he ever strikes
What is: what I owe him and never what he owes me

For $1000: How I carry what he has given me

What is: like a carry-on cutting into my shoulder at the airport
What is: like new weight, stubborn, gathering into a hill
    at the base of my belly

What is: like a twenty-two-pound bag of ice, my hands smarting
in protest if I hold it, really hold it
What is: like a toddler who sometimes wants me to be gentle
and other times wants to be thrown
up into the sky
What is: like my mother carried me, swollen with another
body's
need and feeding it, still feeding
the damn thing
What is: like a bindle, because I will always be without
a home

SECTION II

Can I Go On?

Yes, the Trees Sing

Our backyard's weeping willow is really a woman
with micro braids, all the way down to her waist.
And if you're close enough, you can hear her hummin'

some Dr. Dre. Or is it a drop-top bumpin'
that Jay-Z—*ain't the case, see, it's a matter of taste.*
Our backyard's weeping willow is really a woman

submitting to sound—a trumpet's warble, the strummin'
cha-cha of fingers moving at a jittering pace.
And if you're close enough, you can hear her hummin'

a song you thought you lost; the low-down drummin'
of your mother's palm against your coffee table's face.
Our backyard's weeping willow is really a woman

that reminds you of her. How you knew a storm was comin'
when her hair was disarranged, blown from its place.
And if you're close enough, you can hear her hummin'

a warning siren, the type that has me runnin'
to the porch for her hand before the first cloud breaks.
Our backyard's weeping willow is really a woman
and if you're close enough, you can hear her. Hummin'.

This *Kill Bill* Scene Has Me Thinking About Weave and Girl-Fights

The camera lingers for a moment on the black
flame of O-Ren Ishii's hair in the snow, just sheared
by the bride's Hattori Hanzo, and I think
about what it means to draw hair in a fight. To hitch

a braid or a track from another woman's scalp.
What would our grandmothers say if they knew
we'd forsaken the old proverbs—*Where is my Vaseline?*
or *Bitch, hold my earrings.* These days, victory depends on:

- Grip strength, how well we crook our nails
  beneath the cornrows, how much we loosen
  the black thread holding the extensions

- The strength of the first tug

- Drag distance

- The size of the hole the asphalt eats
  into the other girl's jeans.

Somebody yells out Worldstar, starts recording,
and the crowd's collective flash is hot as stage lights.
Someone's nose is knuckled to spit and blood.
A lip bellies around a cut. A Black girl's bruises

gray under white light. And when the girls are pulled
apart, pieces of themselves left behind
on the other's shirt like O-Ren's slit of blood
in winter's fresh down, the judges must decide

on a loser. The phones record a tracking shot
to the clump of hair or braids on the pavement,
zoom in. The cameras linger on the weave yanked
from owner and updo, and the crowd's uproar

is something like exit music. But we know
this is no samurai's death. No one lives this down.

South Side (II)

So there's nowhere to run, nowhere for us to cry
when the neighbors know your business—the women cooking
on their balconies and patios to side-
eye all the young folks slinking past *Just looking*

how they look. But this is a form of love as well,
the way they judge the length of your daisy dukes
and feed you, send you home with a plate, say, *Tell
your momma I said hello*. They'll put extra scoops

of macaroni and cheese and greens with juice
that will spill into the plastic bag no matter
which way you hold it because the tin foil's loose.
As you tote it home, the juice will leak and splatter

on your leg, drip down your calves, get sticky, dry
a spidered map beginning at the top of your thigh.

The Gathering Place—Grandma's House

I.

Her black piano
keys gummed up from our sticky
fingers. The board aged
from touch; notes shy, delayed,
untuned. Our play made her stop.

Her bedsheets aqua
blue, an ocean of satin
shared with her swollen
limbs. We slept curled on our sides—
a tight line of small cashews.

Her teal tub with white
streaks. My teenage salt dried down
the sides, rimmed the jet
holes like a margarita glass—
toes and heel cast in the tub.

The upstairs bedroom
we all owned once, the Barbie
sheets that unsexed me
in puberty, the dazzling doll
eyes that watched me touch myself.

II.

The gossip spills like
gravy on Christmas linens—
elbow nudges, quick
under-the-table kicking
when the grown folks say too much.

Cousins disappear
to hotbox weed by the park,
sneak back thick as thieves
doused in cologne, smacking gum,
all red-eyed, loose-limbed, loose-lipped.

You still with that boy?
pairs nicely with Chardonnay.
The aunt on her third
marriage says, *The key is sex*,
lifts her glass, toasts to no one.

My grandma absolves
our sins with forehead kisses
and pound cake. *You my
child*, she tells only
me, our little secret. *Mine.*

Sunday Service

"The Blood Still Works" stampedes throughout the nave,
and once the organ player's shoulders seize
with song, the spirit hits the pews in waves.
I catch the loosening necks, the mouths' new ease

in moving before they start to speak in tongues;
I move my lips, pretend to be saved. Right next
to me, my grandma starts to convulse—the drums
of the band, a puppet master or a hex—

and ushers in white surround her, lock their hands
to keep her in. The preacher's sermon lilts
into a screech, his sinners flitter fans
like mosquito wings, and with his eyes he guilts

me into praying hands. I repent for things
I've yet to do. They jerk to tambourines.

Tender-Headed

I resume my Saturday night post
between stretchmarks,
shoulders caught between chestnut
thighs as Grandma greases my scalp.
She carmines the nape of my neck
with her rattail comb, the one
with gaps where my naps
wrestled and won.

The coffee table muddles with jars
of gel and rubber bands that welted
her thumbs when they snapped,
my backside numb on the living room
carpet, dahlia fibers honeycombing
my skin through my oversized tee.

Be still now, and I strain
against her grip on my roots,
chawing tongue to check my
mewls, focusing on the click
of her short nails colliding
as she plaits piece over piece.

She hums "For Your Glory,"
parts my hair into sections,
gridding out old city streets
and rows of cotton;
I wonder if she braids my hair
for the pastor's approval
or God's—they'd never say.

Wreckage

My first instinct was always to sink the ship, my earliest bubble baths strewn with foam glaciers. The blue rubber yacht nameless in water dark with my own dirt. Even young, I was gravity, a soft mass pulling tides from the tub floor. And the boat rode the choppy waters for a while, smooth as a trainer breaking in the newest horse. I knew only of my own joy, my own version of events—the ship captainless and unmanned, no faces painted in its porthole windows. The thing still whole when it hit the bottom. My mother towed it from the water, wet-sleeved, nearly trading her wedding ring to the half-suds snaking the surface. She flipped it upside down and emptied it, held it back out to me. *Again*, as I splashed water onto her neck, clear freckles across her glasses. I pushed the boat back under the water like the head of someone I loved but did not like. *Again*, I screamed.

Now, the ship changes shape and color every time I remember it—first a red and white steamer, then a neon yellow speedboat, finally a blue yacht once more. The water in the tub clear as the vanity mirror, freshly Windexed. Sometimes the boat comes with a small cast of characters, coin-sized dolls and their accessories to lose in the wreckage. Sometimes the boat can come apart in my hands. My mother is close then far—cross-legged on the toilet or toweling her face clean of the day's grease at the sink. Most times, on her knees, the top half of her body cast over the tub's edge as she plays pretend. *This one can be me, and this one can be daddy*, as she places two figures on the small deck. And this time *she* sinks the boat, a gulp where it disappears. Arms wet to the elbows. In this version, I hear the muted clink of her wedding ring hitting the bottom, and when I reach for it she stops me. *Leave it there.* The tiny suitcases spill their contents. The couple loses their shoes in the debris. She doesn't sift through what's left behind.

Painted Tongue

After a while, I find beauty
in bruising, its iridescence,
the way color dates the hurt—
I tell myself that love is touch
that darkens, bears a purple
Salpiglossis with a yellow navel,
spotted and spreading.

In dreams, my father gives me new
jewelry. A tender necklace where his thumbs
would touch below my neck—
a second clavicle, another type
of permanence—or a bracelet
like a clip with teeth or claws.

In the mirror, I'll twist and turn,
sweep my hair back, show my mother—
aren't they gorgeous? She will touch her own
gems, opal or pearls, swivel in the light
until they seem to sparkle.

The saying goes, *Like mother like
daughter.* What then, if mother
is rag doll, fresh canvas to ink?
We twist and turn in the mirror,

my mother and I becoming each other,
her bruises and scars passed down,
family heirlooms that will take

me decades to stop wearing,
~~to sell~~.

Although

Although my mother always knocked
on my bedroom door, *privacy*
was still a bitter word, tasting
foreign in my mouth. I had a lock

on my bedroom door. *Privacy*
was made of only silent letters, the feel of it
foreign in my mouth. I had a lock-
shaped scar across my cheek. The discolored skin

was made of only silent letters, the feel of it
like moth-eaten leather. My mother hated the lock-
shaped scar across my cheek. The discolored skin
a reminder of the accident, the iron-cord in my small hand

like moth-eaten leather. My mother hated the lock-
down of my grandmother's house, the kitchen's busy mornings
a reminder of the accident; the iron-cord in my small hand,
my toddler strength enough to pull the hot iron

down. Of my grandmother's house, the kitchen's busy mornings
were the most dangerous. No one (mothers, aunts) could see me,
my toddler strength enough to pull the hot iron
down to kiss my face. The minutes that passed

were the most dangerous. No one (mothers, aunts) could see me,
where the metal burned me. Someone cradled me, bent
down to kiss my face. The minutes that passed
were filled with blame. *There isn't enough room for privacy.*

Where the metal burned me, someone cradled me, bent
my swollen flesh in their fingers for examination. Their eyes

were filled with blame. There isn't enough room for privacy
even now. I fear my mother bursting in on me and my lover,

my swollen flesh in their fingers for examination, their eyes
closed as they run their lips along the edges of me, my eyes on the door.
Even now I fear my mother, bursting in on me and my lover,
although my mother always knocked.

SECTION III

Poppy Girls

A Diagram with Hands

My aunt tells me, *Those hips are screaming*
      for twins and I want to stop

her at "screaming." I cannot think of a time
      when I wasn't conditioned

to think that this carrying was beautiful.
      My mother likened her pelvis

to a butterfly as my brother flowered
      in its pocket, demonstrated

its spreading with her hands—two flat
      palms cambering into

a shallow bowl. *The body makes room*, she said,
      and waited for me to copy her

movements. I think about this now as my aunt
      mimes an hourglass around

my hips, the image of my mother's cupped
      hands in front of me. How

it was more of a gesture of supplication
      than accommodation,

how instead of life I'd hoped for rain
      in the gourd of her lined palms,

how I wanted only a fresh drink to fill me up.

How to Pray

Each morning, I give
myself over to the scale's

neon complaint, my weight
blazing against my ankles.

The air-conditioning, a choir
of judgment. A friend texted

me to say that what we allow
to dictate our days, we worship—

does that make this square of glass
a god? I suppose this is something

like the Catholic mass, the praying quiet
enough to hear a fresh hymnal

broken in, the first signs of wear
veined into the cover. The scale ticks

and calculates like the priest, his face
checkered with small crosses through

the confessional booth divider.
And I came here to repent, to say

I haven't been eating right. I'll do
more vegetables, more green, I promise

to do better this time. The scale's manual
said nothing of blessings, damnation.

Yet I find both in every
fluctuation, my body telling on

me. I went heavy on the carbs last
night, a pint of ice cream melting

as fast as I could down it. *Repent,*
a red warning before I let the morning

in. There in the dark, it never
blinks about forgiveness.

South Side (III)

A spidered map beginning at the top of your thigh,
drawn by the fingers of a boy you know
is up to no good. And now he's trying to ply
you open in a back seat with his sly talk—*No*

one has to find out. For days, the smell of leather
will mean *home.* The sound of your sweaty back unsticking
like Velcro, your only claim on him. *We together*
or not?—after a week of this, of him licking

his fingers after he dips into you like a jar
of honey. Of course he isn't yours to keep.
He'll come for one of your girls too, pull his car
up to your stoop and offer her a "ride" in his Jeep

like he hasn't had you too. And what can you say?
He was only taught the game, and all he knows is play.

Cloud Watching

It started out innocent enough.
The two of us just falling into our bodies
like new skaters, not yet in high school. At the park
one day, you created a new game. *Let's watch the clouds, just*

the two of us. Just falling into our bodies,
we saw parts of ourselves in the sky tangling with parts of each other.
One day, you created a new game. *Let's watch the clouds, just*
touch me here. No one is watching. What about what

I saw? Parts of ourselves in the sky tangling with parts of each other,
the curl of your lip when I said, *I'm not ready, don't*
touch me here. No one is watching. What about what
I still remember? How the rain saved me, soured

the curl of your lip? When I said, *I'm not ready, don't*
hurt me, you grew through me like weeds.
I still remember how the rain saved me, soured
the blanket beneath us. How years later, when I said, *You*

hurt me, you grew through me like weeds
with your anger. Redid the scene. Your fists clutching
the blanket beneath us—*How?* Years later, when I said, *You*
don't love me, you tried to convince me of the opposite

with your anger. Redid the scene. Your fists clutching
my hair. The hem of my dress. The strap of my bra. You
don't love me. You tried to convince me of the opposite
back when we were kids. You caressed

my hair, the hem of my dress, the strap of my bra. You
revealed your true self when you described the clouds.
Back when we were kids, you caressed
the sound of *take* and *hard* in the mouth,

revealed your true self when you described the clouds
as me *liking it rough*. Now I hate
the sound of *take* and *hard* in the mouth,
the way people misunderstand the story. How they see it

as me "liking it rough." Now I hate
when they say, *Oh honey. He didn't know better. You have to show them
the way.* People misunderstand the story. How they see it—
it started out innocent enough.

Paying for Hotels

Hotel beds are about what is left

behind; side profiles molted from sweat,

makeup left on white shore, earrings snagged

from their holes, mashed into the mattress

with the weight of bodies like pins

into a bulletin board. If you ran a Blacklight

over these sheets, I'm sure you'd find

my shame. I paid for the king bed,

more space for you to spread

me, to find where the sheets had gone cold

and heat them again. I paid for the king

bed to sleep alone in the middle and to feel

for what you left with my hands:

a sock trapped at the foot

of the bed, your belt, waistless,

a black snake slithering into my touch.

What have you found in your own

bed? Nude-colored underwear, a hair

tie, maybe even a warm body some nights,

none of them belonging to me.

When in the Wendy's Drive-Thru, They Ask Me What Sauce and I Say

honey mustard and regret it
because it was your favorite.
Just last month or the month
before, honey mustard tear-
dropping into your beard as
we ate on your leather couch,
the sauce like a thick dusting
of pollen over the bramble.
And you, a first sign of spring.
Then my thumb braving
the sharper bristles to catch
what begged for your white
T-shirt. Your teeth caught
my finger, nipped its pad
before I could return it to my
own tongue to taste you. *Mine,*
you said. *All mine.* A part of me
disappearing into your
mouth. And what about
the other time, when
honey barbeque clung
to your chin's steel wool
until you covered my body
with yours in my bed? You
humming Kendrick Lamar
into the bowl of my clavicle,
how I was the swimming pool
you wanted to dive in.
You called it art afterwards—
your beard's accidental
stippling—sauce swirling

across my upper breast,
Van Gogh's *Starry Night*
remixed. Your breath
as smoky as a summer camp
bonfire as you cleaned the plate
of me, said *You've never
tasted sweeter.* Now I spill sauce
onto myself in my apartment,
shirtless. Honey mustard needles
down my sternum gap,
and there is no one to reclaim
these grasslands. No one
to stop me before I dab
away the mess, to say *I got it*
and let their dinner go cold.

Dream in Which You Cuff Me to the Bed

And your voice segregated itself from the masked darkness, your
    sung commands peeling themselves from the box fan purr-
    ing in the corner. The last command nailed into the junction
    where my wrists meet,
And you joked that I was like a cross of flesh, divine in how my
    body's rippling furnished your hands with warmth,
And every touch was feathered with play, with tease,
And there was a fine line between marking what belonged to you
    and marking what tried to escape your possession,
And when you think about it, there is no difference between
    the two,
And so you landscaped a field of pink weeds across the tops of my
    thighs and the skin swelled in the cool after-sting, an insinua-
    tion of a wound,
And then the blood in quick remission,
And you gently whipped new rib lines, red as a lip freshly bitten,
    because it all started with the ribs, you said,
And even this ignorance was biblical, the way I saw nothing, knew
    nothing until you were a serpent and fruit was waiting on my
    tongue,
And I remembered you had wild ideas about pleasure—said the
    body usurps the self,
And it was less that and more magic, a bewitching of fingers and
    friction
And it was less that and more exorcism, the bend of my back only
    half-human when the thing leaves me,
And once you said this moment after was like having a house in
    the suburbs, that after the hard yard work you must tend to the
    flowers, their stems beginning to curve as they strain for light
    on the kitchen sill,
And I wake from this dream hot with noon, the day bucketed and
    kicked over, spilling into the room,
And behind my sleep mask, I turn my face towards the sun.

Men Really Be Menning

On Dating

I. The Tinder Guy

It's the way you greet me, that crotch-grab cockiness
typed out and framed in a Tinder message saying
Girl, what that mouth do? And since you asked, it's obvious
you've imagined it—me on my knees and praying

to the hymn of a jingling belt, the thirsty pink
tongue of me cropped up towards your warmth. I bet
you're the type who likes control, a girl on the brink
of choking you down, the glitter-glisten of wet

eyes begging for mercy. I wonder who has swiped
right and unhinged their jaw for you, you who
would tell me to say your name while mine was wiped
from memory, my number never saved. Undo

it all, reverse the words and feel them bloat
on the swallow, let it revolt in the back of the throat.

II. The Collector

On the swallow, let it revolt. In the back of the throat
I try to hide the sharpest edge of myself—
the tongue, corkscrewed around the names I hope
to call you when we part. You grapple a wealth

of my backside like you own it on our first
date. Out in the open too, in the line at the movies—
some pissing contest, a macho gesture birthed
from your entitlement. I use the term *own* loosely

because it isn't *me* you want to keep,
only the keepsakes I'll leave behind—the earring,
the hair tie, the panty-proof still buried deep
between the headboard and mattress gap, me leering

at the camera in a photo, naked, spread
according to your directions, splayed on your bed.

III. The Guy Who Has Nothing to Offer

According to your directions, splayed on your bed
is *where a woman looks her best*—at least,
that's what your bio says on Bumble. I read
your list of requirements, your perfect woman pieced

together in bullet points; *gotta be thick,*
shorter than me, willing to hold me down,
no kids cause I got my own, want more. I click
through photos, your curated existence—the brown

of your face half-ghost behind the smoke of a blunt;
you, posed at a bar, a Solo cup suspended
between your lips; you in the bathroom mirror, the front
of your sweatpants on full display like you intended,

your imprint a trap to stumble into. All
you can promise—a mouth that always tastes of alcohol.

IV. The Taker

You can promise a mouth that always tastes of alcohol
and think it a blessing. Once, at a concert, my date
got I-see-two-of-you drunk from shots of Fireball
and begged for me to kiss him. He didn't wait

for my jaw's relaxing, the gentle invitation
for more, and this is just another story
of being opened, another thing that's taken
from me. He smiled and glimmered in the glory

of disco lights like a boy who found a cheat
code, like a boy who beat the game. *I tasted
like medicine didn't I*, over the steady beat
of my body's warnings. Oh the nights I wasted

believing what I was told—that I'd said yes,
that I was asking for it by wearing that dress.

V. The Taker Covers His Crimes

That I was asking for it by wearing that dress
is debated in the group chat with your boys,
but of course you twist the story, put on your best
innocent act. *But there was so much noise,*

I never heard her tell me no. It's funny
how you ignored my other revolts; the clamp
of my thigh, your fingers crabbing to the honey
pot that you swore was dripping, sweet and damp

against the cotton I wore to ward you off;
how suddenly I had a sister who was home
when you asked to come inside again; your scoff
as I dodged your parting kiss; your drop top's chrome

glistening white in the moonlight, empty; how
I still don't know your last name even now.

VI. The Never-Getting-Nowhere Guy

I still don't know your last name even now,
after a month of pointless small talk. Each
morning, the same *Inception*-like beginning, *How
did you sleep?* before your long and practiced speech,

how you *tossed and turned and could have slept much better
but there's always tonight to try again.* Color me psychic
because I guess your every move, can measure
the distance growing between us like a hyphen

doubling into an em dash. You never make plans,
never find time to call, just text. I become a box
to check, something to occupy those restless hands
you won't shut up about. My wordy blocks

of banter dwindle down to phrases, silence.
What did I do? You ask too late for guidance.

VII. The Hopeful

What did I do? you ask. Too late for guidance
or backup from my girls, I do the unthinkable;
tell you the truth. I hate the stretch of silence
that goes unexplained some nights, the fictional

scenarios I conjure up; the back
room of a club, a woman straddling your lap
naked and grinding, your name on her matte black
lips; or your body glossed in sweat, the slap

of your skin against another's. Instead of calling
me crazy, you adjust, check in on busy nights,
phone in on slow ones. I fall asleep to the stalling
of your breathing on the line. You take two flights

to see me and the first touch leaves me bodiless—
it's the way you greet me, that crotch-grab cockiness.

In Flashes

Your mother's house. Your childhood
bedroom. Past midnight, mere hours
before a Sunday sermon. Your popcorn
ceiling transformed, a face laughing

at me. My legs butterflied outward
beneath the pin of your body. A warm
pair of handcuffs. No, just your hands
around my wrists. My body fanned,

a cross for nailing. The whisperings
of torn lace. A reluctant pooling around
your fingers. Half-moons of teeth-
marks the color of plums. The sapphire

wash of the TV's no-signal screen—the blue
of your face in my dreams. The salt
of you dripping into my eyes. The sting
and blindness. Then rain, the sky's

regurgitation of our offerings. A prayer
to the storm—*take the power, take
the lights, take it all away.* Your hand
a clap of thunder over my mouth.

The Mercy Hour

A Burning Haibun

after Torrin A. Greathouse

After rough nights, we sleep without touching, dream of what we should have said in place of what we didn't. But mercy finds us in the embryonic dawn. The sheets bunch like details in a Bernini sculpture. The light through the curtains, egg-carton gray. Unseen, you silence your work alarm. Find handfuls of me under the covers. Say, *Do you think we have enough time?* Half-asleep, I open. We rock into a frenzy quietly, as if children are in the next room. I wet a silhouette of my back onto fresh sheets. I keep my eyes closed, let my body begin the forgiving. When we are done, the playing field has been leveled. You pepper my collarbone with your *sorry*s, and I line your neck with mine.

When you go shower, the sun is a voyeur. I lay out to dry while it bakes your remains into my skin.

After rough nights ████ without touching
████ we should have ████
████ mercy ████
in the ████ sheets
████ ████.
████

████ silence ████. Find ████
████ me under the covers. ████

████ rock into a ████
████ wet ████ silhouette
of ████
████ forgiving.
████ we are done ████ playing ████

████ sorry ████

████

*

Unseen, you silence ████
me ████ into a frenzy, ████ wet.
your *sorrys* ████ remain ████

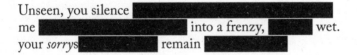

SECTION IV

Ease on Down the Road

South Side (IV)

He was only taught the game, and all he knows is *play
hard at all times.* Once, when he skinned his hands
scarlet, his daddy threatened him, said *I'll lay
you out if you start that crying.* He had plans

for that boy, wanted to raise him numb enough
to lose and keep on living. His friends too, teasing
his quivering lip, testing his manhood with rough-
housing and headlocks so tight they stall the breathing

and bruise the neck. The usual chant—*tap out
and you're a bitch.* Don't let them tell the block
he can't hang, that he's soft. No room for doubt.
He holds his breath, gets strong enough to knock

the other boys on their backs. Passes this down
to those who come after. This is the law of the town.

If I Could Love Life into Him

On the tip of a tongue one note following another
is another path, another dawn where the pink sky is
the bloodshot of struck, of sleepless, of sorry, of
senseless, shush.

—CLAUDIA RANKINE,
"In Memory of Trayvon Martin"

My own name cuts through
the night like ceiling fan blades, pulls
me from a dream. And again,
until my brother's silhouette
fills my bedroom doorway like
a murderer's. But he doesn't yet have
the posture to kill, his preteen body
still prototyping danger, laying bone
and muscle like concrete.

He can't sleep, so he roots
his mattress from its frame, drags
it across the carpeted hall into my room,
one long *shhhhhh* as the mattress
irons a path. On the floor beside me, his breathing
stutters as if he is restarting from
a nightmare. I tell him everything about
nothing, how tonight's full moon

spits white against my car
in the driveway, how Chicago snow
will turn the emptied tree
branches to drooping mustaches
in a matter of weeks. His body gives
the tears away—all its shuddering—
so I slink down beside him,

become a second blanket. I am struck
that it has been over a decade
since I have held him, since he has cried
in my arms. He peels his wet face
from the front of my shirt,
tilts it upwards towards me to say

something, and I wish I could see his
eyes. I want to know if they are now pink
skies, if what has always been clear is now
the color of water that has washed
the hands of a killer.

How Young Boys Survive the Ghetto: 101

after Ghetto Boy, Chicago, Illinois *by Gordon Parks, 1953*

Play house. Climb on a chair of shit-stained paisley
in an alley, avoid the broken bottles. Cut
your momma's housedress, make a cape that's maybe
a size too big. Pose for this camera, strut

like the pimps that limp these streets in zoot suits, caned
and gold-toothed. Know the power of a stuck-out
hip, its demand for respect. Practice your slang,
and call the women *shorties* until you luck out,

get slapped upside the head. Don't turn around.
Don't look behind and see the world's kept going,
that Eldorado dropping down to the ground,
its rims still spinning, pool-hall lights still glowing—

boy look into this lens, let me remember you
like this, carefree, acting a fool like you always do.

mother

noun (1)

moth·er | \ 'mə-thər \

1: a female parent
2: maternal tenderness or affection
3: [short for *motherfucker*] sometimes vulgar

—*Merriam-Webster*

I have not yet been split
by motherhood,

have not yet felt my body
become sick with

itself, relinquished of its
own parts—the

lips that have latched on
to me, I needed

in a different way. Yet I
hurt the way a

mother hurts; stretch-marks
like tendons,

like ribbons piecing me
together, heavy

breasts like water balloons
that never burst

on contact, gifts I refuse
to open.

*

My body knows something
I don't, like how

to take up space, how to
fill a hole. I slip

into the hands that call for me
at dusk, when

the hour knows no difference
from *mother* or

sister or *daughter*. Hips can
bear the sins

of others too—perhaps this
is what tips

the scale, those morsels of *sorry*
and *hold me*

I collect from bathroom floors
and bedsides.

*

The first time *motherfucker*
felt like anything,

it was my father calling my
mother the name,

thrown over his shoulder
like salt after he

spilled it in restaurants—an exit
wound. My mother

bore it painfully at first, then
quietly, sort of like

giving birth—once you tear
all the way through,

everything feels like nothing,
and nothing hurts.

Don't Go Getting Nostalgic

Some years there exists a wanting to escape—
you, floating above your certain ache

—CLAUDIA RANKINE, *Citizen*

When cleaning my family home for the sale, I excavate memories, some
crumpled paper-portals into flashbacks. In my nightstand drawer, years
of notes I smuggled through theology classes, and my signature barely
    there
at the ends of diary entries, the pages golding like teeth. Another me exists
in my childhood bedroom, still thin enough to worm beneath the bed. A
version of me that still believes that loving you was enough, that wanting
things to work would make it so. In a big manila envelope labeled
    "Letters to
Grief," my sixteen-year-old self wishes herself dead, probes a different
    escape
route in each dispatch. And then your love notes, your scribbled *I love you*
on every letter stuffed in the old pencil case, your pen-doodled roses
    floating
in the margins of your promises—*We'll never be apart.* And I'm not above
crying over long-lost things, but this is where it gets embarrassing. Your
name starts to bring tears to my eyes in grocery store aisles. And when I
    hear certain
songs, I miss something I've forgotten the name of. What a special kind
    of ache.

A Cut Foot Teaches Kindness

I cradle my foot like an infant's in my grip,
a red-lipped kisser daggered into its sole
and glass still rooted in flesh—a crystal wing tip
to tweeze loose, gently. Slowly. It makes a hole

too deep to dam with pressure, my T-shirt's hem
pressed to the wound, a poor man's gauze, soaked through.
Last week, I called my mother on a whim
and asked her how she dealt with loneliness. *You*

learn to take care of yourself, become your own
Prince Charming. So I extract the shard like a lover
might, ask myself—*Does it hurt? You alright?*—along
the way. I'd kiss it if I could reach. I'd cover

it with my lips and say, *There there.* If healing
was as easy as this, I could get used to the feeling.

Drunken Monologue from an Alcoholic Father's Oldest Daughter

My friends say I should have been a therapist and it ain't funny
no more. I ain't seen a dollar of pay for this labor, all my
    pretending—
who do I see about my check? My father says, *I just need somebody
to talk to* when he calls. He's sitting in our house alone
looking at old pictures and drinking. *I still love my wife, I still love
my wife.* And if I answer the phone, I gotta be the mother

he missed out on as a kid. I pick up and I gotta turn on a mother's
softness. But I ain't gave birth to nothing. Never felt that funny
feeling of my second self latching on to the first. How do you love
something that looks right through you? You gotta pretend,
act like you understand. My father says, *I spent Christmas alone
for the first time in my life* and man I swear somebody

needs to give me an Oscar for the way I sounded like somebody's
momma. Said, *God gon' work it out.* But I know my mother
did the right thing. Left him. My brother and sister were alone
with him for hours while she was gone, and I, you know, I just felt
    funny
about it. And the way my father would call me pretending
he was the victim when I knew what it really was. Maybe we all loved

the chaos a little bit, having a place to put the blame. Maybe I loved
the way they needed me. But I ain't love the pressure. Somebody
told me that I was the glue that held it all together. Now I gotta
    pretend
that's a compliment, I gotta "ha-ha" and "he-he" when they call me
    "mother
2.0." I laugh and say *I don't even need kids anymore* but what's so funny
about that, a hatred that spreads to the womb? I've had a lot of alone

time to wonder about the choices my father makes. Being alone
over rehab, over family. Sometimes I say, *That motherfucker don't love
me* to myself in the mirror real tough. And I keep saying it until it's
>   funny,
until I'm laughing and then I'm crying and then I sound like somebody
dying when I start coughing from both. Sometimes I ask my mother
what happened to him and she just says *it's sad.* Most times, I pretend

I feel the same and I *mhm* on the phone but this time I can't pretend
no more. I say, *Momma, I know you feel bad for leaving him alone
but it was the right thing to do.* I say, *You did what any mother
would have done.* I say, *The kids know you did it out of love,
to protect them.* She silent, so I say, *Momma, he could have killed somebody*
and she says, *Hardy-har-har, real funny.* But just how funny

if we ain't laughing? I want to say something in the silence, some-
>   thing funny,
but I know my mother wants to be left alone when she pretends
to yawn. So I tell her I love her. And I don't remember who hangs up.
>   Somebody.

The Therapist Asks Me, "What Are You Afraid Of?"

I think of the word *hunger*, both a noun
and something my hands are capable of.
How my parents made a little god

of me when they fed them, placed a snow
globe in my palms' chalice. Inside the dome,
a sleeping city I'd shake awake, shake back

to their hurting—I promise there's an answer
to your question in here somewhere. Every
night, I whipped the glitter into a storm

and the same small figurines grasped
at one another in the cold; nothing changed
this. Some nights, I wound the metal key

for a lullaby and when no one danced,
I questioned my own God. I played the shrill
song until it yawned into a dirge

or some sort of warning, and I would say
that maybe this is a metaphor for life, or love,
but I know you'd make sure to write

that down. And you're nodding because
you're so sure you know where this is going—
yes, sometimes even our most precious things

can slip through our fingers. When I shattered it,
I couldn't make a noise. A wisp of the music
box's song escaped the glass like a spirit,

there was no difference between the feeling
of water and blood beneath my feet. You leaning
forward like this is gossip (and this too

is another way to hunger) but my life was
changed. I stepped right into the glass because
I thought that would be the worst part,

and it wasn't. Knifed an ugly tree into the sole.
My scars grew fruit that scabbed over, dropped
in the new season. The remembering hurt

more than the living because shame dials
in. You hearing me? I was naive enough
to think I could control a life. Even mine.

SECTION V

Emerald City Sequence

I Spy

I walk outside through my apartment complex once the sun has set and the eye of Birmingham's heat has been switched off. Some residents walk their dogs beneath the flittering lampposts, leave the shit behind to be stepped in, to cast someone's footprint in tomorrow's bake. Others sit on their balconies, uncap whatever IPA was on sale at the Fresh Market. The caps kiss the concrete like loose change. I come out at night mainly to watch the trees, their night-time transformations. How when I stand beneath them and look up at the sky, the branches look like fingers culling the sky for pearls of light. How the moon cracks like a white porcelain plate behind their cover. I look for everything I've ever known in the bare branches; the frayed fibers of heat-damaged hair, the cartography of a river splitting, its distributaries like offspring on a family tree. Tonight, I find the silhouettes of the teenaged boys who walked my block in Chicago's South Side. During the summers, they cycled through different colored tank tops, and every night they anchor-chained home, all branch and switch. *Shit* and *damn* were Jolly Ranchers in the mouth, syruping with the warmth of their spit. The wet tanks on their backs a second, pinched skin. Blood weeded to a surface. And I never knew where they came from. It was almost as if they'd sprouted from darkness itself—pushing up through the cracks of the broken sidewalks then duplicating—their shadows twinning like background dancers in the moonlight.

South Side (V)

To those who come after, this is the law of the town—
the South Side is not a place, but a state of being,
a song, the candy lady circling around
the blocks with walking tacos, Kool-Aid unfreezing

in Styrofoam cups. Happiness costs so little
for those who are willing to buy. And everyone
has a name; the man who drives the ice-cream truck, the nickel-
and-dime bag boys with Frootie Rolls lining one

side of their jackets' insides—Mr. Bradley,
Joshua 'nem, their presence steady as statues.
How much of this city is flavor? The thick and sappy
taste of too sweet, too quick to melt, the cashew

crunch of Garrett popcorn mix? It's sensory;
the act of remembering, of making memory.

Club Anthem

To You and Your Boys Watching Me

Song says, *I put my hand upon your hip*,
says, *when I dip, you dip, we dip*, but I

don't know you like that. You detour to the bar
through this ungodly gulch, bodies in cyclone-

swirl, and your fingers groping blind. You slide
behind me, your *excuse me* drowned by the DJ's

instructions—*Drop it low, y'all, touch the flo'*.
I'm twerking, throwing my weight to the beat until

your denimed crotch abrades my backside, then
pressure. A squeeze, you snaking your hips against

the rising hem of my bodycon dress. The fake
surrender always gets me, open-palmed

and wide-eyed. *My bad, my bad*. Boy, gone somewhere.
At the bar, you order a double Jack and Coke

and return to the pack, your boys a cluster of button-
down shirts, Figaro chains, the chewed-down straws

in your drinks stiletto-sharp, scratching your pink
and thirsty tongues. And you watch me, plot a new

route to my bounce, my shake, the pendulum-knock
of your eyes a twin to the rhythm of my ass.

Squeeze by me one more time. I dare you to.

Yellow Dress

after Beyoncé's "Hold Up" music video

I knew you'd come undone / your double-doored entrance an off-print of elevator doors in *The Shining* / water now where blood once swept a hotel hallway // Barefoot / your ankle bracelet fracturing sunlight with its glitz / you carry a river's weight in your dress's pleats // And B / I screamed at the screen when you swiped / the baseball bat from the kid and readied your swing / your full-mouthed smile the cue / to fuck shit up // Your toenails the color of *Redrum* / *Redrum* / *Redrum* // Yoncé show me how to do damage in high heels / how to become a chandelier from a windshield's leavings // *What's worse, B* // *Looking jealous or crazy* // You collapse a passenger window / crack the cap off the yellow hydrant like a home run / and dance in its shower with the neighborhood's children // Watch them high-step through the wake of your rage // You make the town your playground // And sure / the explosions were over the top / but add this scene to the list of women strutting away from what they rightfully destroyed / like Angela Bassett dousing a cheater's clothing and car in gasoline / and lighting her own cigarette to watch it burn // There was no bat / but I set fire to my ex's things the other day / the silver chain of a birthday gift melting down to rainbow / ash // A stack of letters licked by the fire's spreading tongue // I waited beneath the tent of dawn / the flames beginning to swallow themselves / the smell of campfire fixed to my hair like bleach // At the end of your music video / *pop* / you shatter the cameraman's wrist / or beat a hairline fracture into the skull // The world's color bleeds out onto the street.

On Hesitation

I wished I'd let you drive as the sky closed the lid on things.
The headlights on the other side of the highway blurred to
orbs as fuzzy as dandelions, my sight failing in the dark.
But I was in a groove, wasn't ready to stop again before
we crossed the next state line. So when you spotted a
barn—a black stamp licked and pressed against the mid-
night blue—I stopped you before you even began. *We don't
have time for adventures.* But this pattern continued, you
straightening at each sighting of wood-rot, at every front
barn door cracked open like a knife wound. Soon, I tired of
the cornfields. Their sameness, the vanity with which they
continued to spawn the self. So I indulged you, abandoned
the highway's smooth to spit gravel in the wake of your
Jeep. When we pulled up to this barn, you dated its aban-
donment. *At least ten, fifteen years*, because of the smile of
the roof. The wind breezing through the barn's gut, it's cat-
call whistle, and both sets of doors blown open. Your pulse
two-stepped during our silent watching and I thought you
were turned on by this somehow. And my God, you were.
Let's go in. Find some hay, like in the movies. And what of the
pessimist in me? Betting on the rustic charm of disarray as
a trap, some chainsaw-wielding killer eyeing us from the
cyclops window. Even you could go rogue, one bite of me
giving way to another, then another. But you've gotten out
of the car now, come around and opened my door. *We'll
laugh about this years from now.* Your hand in the dark not
how I always remember it.

Lump

When I was younger, I found a secret in a science book before my mother had a chance to explain it to me herself. In my bedroom, I studied the diagram of what my flat chest would become, how a whole network of fat and feeling would bloom beneath the skin without my permission. In the pictures, the breast was a flower—the lobes like purple petals connected to the light pink nipple. This rendering softened my initial fears of invasion; on the inside at least, this flowering could be beautiful.

After I'd bloomed my mother taught me how to examine my breasts, said, *You should know your body better than anyone.* To demonstrate, she raised her left hand, pressed her left breast with the other hand. Later, alone in my room and in bed, I practiced beneath my oversized T-shirt. The fat of my breast rolled beneath my hand's inquiry. I stirred small circles down to the muscle until I memorized the feeling. I pressed, poked, and pinched until I was sore.

Now, a little after 2 a.m., I palm my left breast the way a man might, find it tender. I let my fingertips ride the dense waves until I hit a bump that does not shift with the rest of the fat. I pass over it from different angles, but the result remains. I rest my palm there as if it will tell me something, introduce itself, and I think of everything the world has said about this part of me. How once before, I Googled "dense breasts" and the internet told me, *Sometimes, it feels like you are made of heavy rope—don't be alarmed.* How my lover says, *I love how they've gotten bigger these past few years* without understanding the consequences of more.

*

I

diagram

This
invasion;
this flowering   .

I
should know   *better*   .

alone
I practice
inquiry

the way a
man might,   tender.   my fingertips

tell me

it feels
heavy   *be alarmed*
say
understand   the consequences   .

SECTION VI

Is This What Feeling Gets?

After the Car Accident

I slow traffic with my worry, kneeling and checking my car for damage. My palm on its feverish hood like a mother checking a child's temperature, and the heat of the sun doubling its sickness. In the black paint's warped reflection, I could be mistaken for my father—this froggish position, squatting on my toes. My forehead becoming his in its rumpled state, even our concern biological, shared, right down to the way we squint at an injured thing. The way we have only temporary fixes for what is broken. I list the damages out loud, to no one, to the metronome of my hazard lights. To convince myself I've done it—this too is hereditary, struggling with admissions of guilt. On the phone with the insurance company, I begin to unbraid a legacy of blamelessness. *Yes, I was operating my vehicle alone. The car was parked and empty when I hit it.* This is just another version of the tree falling in the forest question; if no one saw me hit the car, did I do it? If my father never apologized on our old phone calls, did he truly wound me? The insurance agent on the phone is asking questions, following the printed script taped next to her computer screen. *Is the car drivable? Are you hurt?* I don't know which question I'm answering anymore. It doesn't matter. *Yes.* It comes pouring out of me like smoke from a car's underbelly, the hiss of air finding the path of least resistance. *Yes. Yes. Yes.*

Rooftop Monologue

When I'm not thinking of dying, I like to play
God. Look; from this angle, the world folds

inward like a Monopoly game board,
and those people below are more than just ants

to crush in the pretend-pinch
of my index finger and thumb. See the top

hat and thimble, the boats and silver dogs
backsliding along the sidewalks? I wore my old

Converse today. The soles unstitching
from the canvas, the beginnings of lips

around my toes. Enough flex
in the soles to cuddle the roof's ledge the way

the other woman might hold a man after
a fight with his wife. I don't want to jump,

only to be reminded of how thin the line between
breathing and falling. How fragile a crossing.

With the sun setting like that, it looks like you
could hike uphill right into heaven, these skyscrapers

steps for the giant. And the sky like hand-pulled
cotton candy, sifting into ropes of rose

and gold, stretching and re-stretching itself into
mouthfuls. Listen, I told you I don't want to jump,

but what a view. Watch, the sky is hemorrhaging
twilight—my own creation, too beautiful to ruin.

I won't scatter myself on the sidewalk tonight.

Scripture

You never understood the point, the Word
of God in every hotel nightstand. Thought

it heresy. *Don't they know what happens here?*
It became your secret fascination, logging

the different Bibles we found on road trips, culling
a story from the wear of their spines. *This room*

has seen a whole lot of sinners, when a Bible
undressed itself in your lap. Sometimes, you'd read

the annotations from a previous guest
out loud, an abridged confession in the margin—

I pray my husband can forgive me, next
to Hebrews chapter thirteen, verse four. We were

unmarried, sinners every time you cracked
me open like the good book. My spine its own

story—the bending, the way it rids itself
of cover, how it arches the fullest part

of me into your hands. Our bed is godless
each time you press me into it, and still

you shut me up with your scripture every time;
Don't call on him now. Your Lord can't save you here.

Let Me Call On You

Oh Lord, how I find you in the mundane
pains of the day—a stubbed toe, a pinky finger
nicked, a little blood seasoning the white
onion and cilantro still damp
from their cleaning.

*

I was seven when my cousin and I tore
into the fresh box of Cheez-Its in my grandmother's
pantry and ladled handfuls into
our mouths. When a cracker escaped him,
he pinched it from the linoleum, held it
up to the kitchen light. *God made
dirt, and dirt don't hurt*, he said, popped the orange
square into his mouth. When he didn't chew
I knew he was letting it melt, his spit
turning salt and cheese to mush.

*

My God, what a mess I make
of everything. When a sharp pain cracks
through my left breast I learn to kneel
again, a skill I broke with my hands and left scattered
in the beds of old lovers. I was naive enough to believe
that man was my body's master; he said, *Come,*
and it was so. He said, *This is my body,*
and placed it on my tongue. For a moment
he made me forget I was naked,
that your gaze should make
me want to scramble for
the nearest sheet.

*

When my father drank himself into
the driver's seat of his Infiniti, I called
out *Jesus* and didn't mean *you*. I said *Jesus*
for my mother wrestling the keys out
of the ignition. *Jesus* for the onlookers shaking
their heads, their lips miming a prayer
for the three children in the backseat. *Jesus*
for the way my eyes were glassed moons
in the window's dark mirror. *Jesus* when the taste
of my own salt shocked me
at the corner of my lips.

*

My lover throws away the blood-stained
vegetables, lets the wooden chopping board capsize
in the sink's fresh water. In the bathroom,
he runs my finger under cold water. *Goddamnit*,
when the blood does not dam itself. He applies
pressure over a folded paper towel, and my eyes roll
to the heavens. A pink film dries
around the sink drain.

*

Bandaged and banned from the knife
rack, I watch him finish making the meal, top
the carne asada tacos with the fixings. He presents
my plate with the seriousness of a bishop,
two-handed and careful. We close our eyes to say
grace. *Lord, let this food be nourishing*
to our bodies, I say. *Let nothing in this meal harm*
us, oh God. I open my eyes to find
my lover mid-bite, the tortilla already breaking

in his hands, the juice from the meat
and lime dripping down his chin
like communion that missed
the tongue.

Self-Portrait as Moon Drowning in Petrichor, Which Is to Say My Ribcage Texts While I Drive

The saying goes, *Don't look directly into the sun*, but I remember moon instead. Once, we sat in your car at the lake, watched its face dusk to black ink. There was something about your hands, moon-bleached. I couldn't stop describing things: how the moon was a porcelain plate in the water, how your beard grazed between my thighs in the backseat, how love is a system that can glitch. This was the last time I was honest with myself. The body decides what it wants before I can agree. So when you started skipping stones shirtless, I watched the cables of muscle in your back, their roll and pitch in the headlights. The next time you texted me to meet you here I knew I would wait, and then I would come

again
      and
again
      and
again.

Let Us Do Nothing

On this thousandth
day, God said, *Let there be sky*
as gray as dirty

dishwater. No light
to let in. You needed to
go to the store, but

I expedited
my prayer for a free car
wash. And so it pours,

the world outside our
window a jarful of beads;
capped, jangling. You call

this "first fall," the earth
yawning a cold that doesn't
quite get into the

bones. And I don't know
how to tell you that my knees
predicted this drop

in temperature, my
joints like two church choirs singing
the same note. You throat-

breathe a fog onto
the glass and strike a face through
it. The banana-

curved frown sweating down
to the sill. *Come back to bed,*
I say. *Come to me.*

South Side (VI)

The act of remembering (of making memory)
rebuilds the city in my mind two states
away. The Ohio River cutting simply
across the state line, its surface an empty face

to cough up the mind's desires. The Chicago skyline
undulates into view like a vision, glitters
like a firework mushrooming out against the wine
red of a scramming sky. If water is mirror,

what does that make of me? I call a friend
who lives back home, tell her I miss the heartbeat
of Chicago, the way the skyscrapers seem to bend
down to protect me. I skip a rock to pleat

the water's calm. Yet I still see you there.
The river carries you downstream like a prayer.

SECTION VII

Believe in Yourself

Elegy for Spring

I.

You said it was like being unwound—
a tiny fist cranking you back
into a music box—when the dawn chorus
began each spring morning, an ellipsis
of robins on the sill. You were your truest
self before the covers were thrown
to the foot of the bed, before the sound
of you brushing your teeth scuffed
against the shower water
still drawing heat from the pipes. Still wrapped
in dream-warmth, you said, *Good morning*,
with our mouths nearly touching.
When I tried to squirm away, twittering
with the birds, you held me to you,
smoothed me like a shirt
that needed ironing. Your usual joke—
Two morning breaths cancel
each other out.

II.

In my earliest years, there was
no front lawn. Only plates of concrete,
cracked and shouldering for space.
The first day of spring was never x-ed out
on the calendar, but marked when the ground
was warm enough to grill the fillets
of my bare feet. When we moved to a house
with a lawn, spring came earlier for

us, meant wet grass that dried
by noon. *Golf-course green,*
my father called it when he still held the power
to name things for me.
Our very own golf-course green.

III.

You and I took turns parking in the single-
car garage when we moved in together. Fairness
was what you thought I needed. But really, I envied
the mornings when your car slurped the sun
in the driveway, wished for the warm
that waited for you. You never knew this,
but I stomached this small rage with coffee
until it bent me over. Soured me.
In the winters, you asked, *What have I done?*
I couldn't explain the importance
of the spring morning, how I remembered
my father's gentleness most clearly
in its simmering.

IV.

Winter took everything from me
as a child—the brittle bark that scabbed
my hands after I climbed the tree in the front yard,
the grass's neon coat, my watchful father
on the front porch. With no fireplace,
he found other paths to heat—the refuge
of his bed, my mother's body,
the spill-spread of a beer hitting
the center. And it's true, there is something genetic
about craving. How was I to know

that spring would become like a shot
of whiskey, relenting
what hardened in the colder months?

V.

I was never honest with you,
never admitted why I changed
with the seasons. *You're so damn hot
and cold*, as you packed the last
of your things. Of course you left
when frost still tongued the driveway,
when snow was Wite-Out
on the roofs. For months
I would remember the last time you gifted me
warmth—the slow lap
of your headlights
as I watched you from the doorway.
Oh, how you reminded me
of my father then.

The Way a Chicago Summer Comes

At the tail end
of May, the weather
finally turns on itself
like a mother dog
giving birth, pitched over
on her side, grunting.

Finally, I see summer
pressing at her opening,
its hairless bulb stretching
the skin, popping free,
arriving in a slush
of muck and heat.

I'm afraid to touch
it, to scoop it
up in my hands
and towel the wet
pink from its eyes,
to find it still,
pulseless against me,

until it pokes out
its tongue, the unsticking
of its slick mouth
a relief, an echo
of my unspoken prayers.

On Getting Ate Up by Mosquitoes

The bugs would like to have a word, or maybe
a mouthful of something that moves
when I walk. On the back porch, a baptism
in Off!, one continuous spray
in the sign of the cross, as holy as the soap
grandma exorcises the mouth
with. I break all the "outside" rules. Green up
my white dress with the grass's
open-mouthed saliva. Put on my "smell-good
stuff" so I don't stink
like the fever of an August night breaking.
When night falls, we box
the yard's perimeter with citronella torches.
We stop putting our hands
on each other and start popping ourselves
at the lightest hint of a landing,
dot our palms with unlucky insects. Yet
there are always ones
that I miss—the seasoned few who mastered
the map of my body.
Inside, I count the fresh dunes steeling
in the air-conditioning,
I tell myself that it must be me, that I have
too much for the taking.

South Side (VII)

The river carries you downstream like a prayer,
then you are gone. I compare you to this new
home, where the downtown drivers refuse to blare
their horns at pedestrians, and the nighttime blue

cools down to darkness in degrees. And no
screech of the "L" train snaking above my head,
no roar to drown a conversation. The glow
of the suspension bridge at night; the red

then blue then purple. The standing sign—THE QUEEN
CITY—in front of the Ferris wheel. I learn
to find you everywhere I look, to glean
your shadow from Cincinnati's light and turn

it into home when I feel lost, when I am ailing.
This is what teaches me love—your streets, their wailing.

Conversion

On Cincinnati's Converted Churches, God, and Lucifer

I.

The other day I almost felt the burden
of sin in Urban Outfitters (church of markups, house
of worship for pretenders, the suburban
teens masquerading as city-born). A blouse

on a rack arrests the gem-light from the rose
window, anemic sunlight dribbling through
stained glass, re-pressing new designs. Transpose
Jesus onto the Grateful Dead, skeletons toe-

to-toe and Our Lord and Savior kneeling, washing
their metatarsals. The mannequins wear
it better here, their pseudo-sockets watching
me mime their poses. Fiberglass arms bare

in tank tops. Legs half-lunging. One foot en pointe
like a disciple's, for me to kiss. Anoint.

II.

Like a disciple, for me to kiss (anoint)
your face is to mark you for betrayal. Coffee
cups and carafes, my lipstick print disjoined
from the trellised skin—I leave behind a copy

of my mouth at cafés. I find a shop that sells
lattes and tea in the sanctuary, plays
old rap songs that would clatter like shotgun shells
in a Sunday service's silence. During the weekdays,

the college kids forget themselves and burn
their tongues on dark roasts, mochas spilled, say *shit*
and cross themselves with a caffeinated finger-
gun to the head, the chest, the shoulders. I sit

and mouth *the Father, Son, the Holy Spirit*
with every touch, on beat, like a rap song lyric.

III.

With every touch—on beat like a rap song lyric—
my phone works less and less. The telltale check
of Verizon Wireless bums on its side; a satyric
smirk in vermillion, devil-red. At the tech

desk, the employee tests my touchscreen sensors.
He says, *It's almost gone, you'll need to upgrade.*
I let him rob me. His voice resounds from the center
of the store as if he's preaching the terms of the trade-

in, rules like commandments. Forty dollars a month
to hear another voice, for someone other
than God to speak to me. One hundred up front
to kill the loneliness, to call my mother

some days. Siri records and keeps my confession;
Forgive me, Father, for all our missed connections.

IV.

Forgive me, Father, for all our missed connections—
my late-night pillow-prayer. I've avoided
going to church for months now, my collection
of excuses practiced, preached right back. I'm loaded

with bullshit, Sunday morning sermons spent
in bed, damning myself for sleeping too late.
But I never set the alarm. At night, I repent
by kneeling bedside, all my body's weight

branding my knees with the carpet's pattern.
My comforter clings to the dryer's heat. I say
Let me explain, Lord, but it doesn't matter.
We've been here before—last week, the other day

when my tongue played Judas and betrayed me, slipped
and cursed mid-prayer, abandoned the usual script.

V.

*And cursed! Mid-prayer! Abandoned the usual script
again*—you, venting to your angels, another
tally in red by my name. *A sinner's lip
on that one.* I picture you watching me stutter

another apology. Your angels gather
around to eavesdrop and gossip about my judgment
day. What would you say if you heard the scattered
chitchat, your cherubs deep in their discussion

about my devil-speak? Have I sent angels
to punishment with this mouth? Cartoonish
really—you pointing like a parent, the painful
silence that follows *Go to your room.* Their moonish

eyes closed, hands clasped in prayer, asking you
for forgiveness. I hear angels mess up too.

VI.

For forgiveness, I hear angels mess up too.
My grandma tells me, *An angel fell from heaven
because he started "smelling himself," her new*
expression. *Probably ruined it the second*

he got up there. I wonder if all my dreams
of falling are really just me losing
your favor and forgetting. To me it seems
that life is a game of this-or-that, of choosing

to deny the self or indulge. My grandma reminds
me it's never black and white, but different shades
of gray. *It ain't easy being human. Sometimes
we fail a test, or we pass. There ain't no grades*

for that. Everyone sins. Lucifer even, falling
to hell, the heat beneath us licking. Sprawling.

VII.

To hell, the heat. Beneath us—licking, sprawling—
sunlight unfurling on the asphalt. My mother
and I amble through an outlet mall, sweat stalling
in the underwire of our bras. I smother

her hand in mine, wrestle her into air-
conditioning in Forever 21.
She fans herself with a coupon flyer, her hair
flapping in waves. I make a fleeting run

through the markdowns, neon tags for clearance, half
off. An employee asks if I need assistance
when I hold a shirt to my chest—its skeleton laughs,
a bouquet of roses in its mouth, its twisted

grin in on all my secrets, my darker version.
The other day I almost felt the burden.

To the City I Wish to Get to Know

If the Ferris wheel
is the heart, I know
your pulse. I've ridden it
to the top and seen
the buildings' summits
spike the sundown
gradient like a new piercing.
I thawed in the car's glass
cubicle, your waltz
into spring slow and sensual.
What drug is in these
veins? I want to know
the rush, what turns
the Ohio River to a second
sky, those flickers
of office windows and pill-bottle-
orange streetlights
peppering its surface—tell me,
which constellation
looks like me? Which star
should I follow home?

Dear Moon

When the dark curtains for the bedroom came,
I blacked you out like the night
you fight in. Forgive me, but I'm still working

through it in therapy. Lately, I've been so sudden
with my decisions—cut my braids out
of my head a month early, put a deadline

on a man's love. I'm leaving space for nothing
but blame in the new season, and this here
is no different. I never told you about the great hurt

between us. Me, thirteen and thinking I needed you
to speak back to me. Back then, I skipped my wishes
to you like stones over water. I slept in the overhang

of mornings that relieved your shift. I'm angry
I still don't know what to call the thing between
us. Were you friend, or sister? The first lover

to leave when I became too much? I've surrendered
to the half-truth; men remind me of you. The mixed
messages, you in my bed every night and nothing

ever to say of it. My therapist says I'm projecting
but goes silent when I mention that you've been doing it
to me my whole life. At night, I get moody

in waiting. Anxious for you to ask me
how I've been. Anxious enough to pay someone
to ask me now instead. The harder and fuller truth:

men have abandoned me and I never heard
from you. I was a shadow of a wolf,
whimpering into your blank light. I didn't know

that love was an ancestor of quietude,
that you were still there. Of all things
love, I'm still learning.

Acknowledgments

First and foremost, I would like to thank my mother, my two siblings, and the rest of my family and friends. You all remind me that outside of the page and the poems, I am someone worth loving, worth knowing. You make me human again when I lose myself in the work.

Thank you to my dearest friends and first readers—Jason B. Crawford, Madeleine Corley, Sofia Fey—for loving me enough to keep me honest, for committing to my work as intensely as I do. Your generosity and wisdom have helped shape this book into what it is today and continues to shape who I am constantly becoming as a writer.

Thank you to my UC folks—Nick Molbert, Marianne Chan, Connor Yeck, Paige Webb, Holli Carrell—who saw this book in its earlier form. It was your feedback that moved me closer to my vision for its final form, and I couldn't have done it without you all. To my poetry professors, Rebecca Lindenberg and John Drury, whose classes in which some of these poems came to life and/or were workshopped, thank you for expertise, your encouragement, your continued support of my journey as a writer and scholar.

Thank you to my agent Rena, who believed in this book and did not stop fighting for it until it found a home. Who continues to believe in my abilities as a writer.

Thank you to Soft Skull Press for your care and attention to this manuscript from the very beginning. Your enthusiasm and excitement for these poems in turn made me excited again to return to this book during the editing process. Thank you for choosing it, choosing me.

Thank you to my writing community for reading my work, for buying my books, for coming to events, for giving me chance after chance to connect with you on the page. Without you, I would be nothing.

Thank you to my poetic heroes, especially Patricia Smith, whose words served as a guiding light as I trudged through the dark of these poems.

Thank you to the editors and publications who gave many of the poems in this book their first light:

Frontier Poetry, Lammergeier Mag, The Journal, SWWIM, Iron Horse Literary Review, New Ohio Review, Vulcan Historical Review, Knights Library Magazine, Trampset, VIDA Review, Borderlands Texas Poetry Review, Sundog Lit, Soft Punk Magazine, Hobart Pulp, Perhappened Mag, Alien Literary Magazine, Superstition Review, Flypaper Literary Magazine, TriQuarterly, Drunk Monkeys, Eunoia Review, Southeast Review, and *River Mouth Review.*

And endless love and gratitude to you, for being here with me.

Taylor Byas is a Black Chicago native currently living in Cincinnati, Ohio. She is the first-place winner of the 2020 Poetry Super Highway Contest, the 2020 Frontier Poetry Award for New Poets, and the 2021 Adrienne Rich Award for Poetry. She is the author of the chapbooks *Bloodwarm* and *Shutter*.